SHEET MUSIC

Sheet Music

poems

ROBERT GIBB

Autumn House Press

Autumn House Press Staff

Editor-in-Chief and Founder: Michael Simms
Managing Editor: Adrienne Block
Co-Founder: Eva-Maria Simms
Community Outreach Director: Michael Wurster
Fiction Editors: Sharon Dilworth, John Fried
Assistant Editor: Emily Cerrone
Associate Editor: Giuliana Certo
Media Consultant: Jan Beatty
Publishing Consultant: Peter Oresick
Tech Crew Chief: Michael Milberger
Intern: Alecia Dean

PENNSYLVANIA
COUNCIL
ON THE

Autumn House Press receives state arts funding support through
a grant from the Pennsylvania Council on the Arts, a state agency
funded by the Commonwealth of Pennsylvania, and the National
Endowment for the Arts, a federal agency.

ISBN: 978-1-932870-56-5

Library of Congress Control Number: 2011936838

for Maggie

CONTENTS

IV

V

SHEET MUSIC

THE MUSIC LESSON

for Matthew

Having just unpacked that violin
The color of casked brandy
And set it upright before him,
My son starts reciting the names

Of the parts he is learning,
Pointing each one out to his mother
As if tracing a splendid anatomy—
Neck, finger-board, bridge—

The shaped grain gleaming like parquetry
There by the parlor window
Where the words fall like light—
Body, peg-box, scroll—

The taut strings plinking one by one
As he fingers them
In an off-key pizzicato
And goes on with the naming—

Chin-rest *and* tail-piece—
The hours on their way towards him,
The bow he'll soon be using
To kindle music from the chambered wood.

I

KITES

Come March we'd find them
In the five-and-dimes,
Furled tighter than umbrellas
About their slats, the air

In an undertow above us
Like weather on the maps.
We'd play out lines
Of kite string, tugging against

The bucking sideways flights.
Readied for assembly,
I'd arc the tensed keel of balsa
Into place against the crosspiece,

Feeling the paper snap
Tautly as a sheet, then lift
The almost weightless body
Up to where it hauled me

Trolling into the winds—
Knotted bows like vertebrae
Flashing among fields
Of light. Why ruin it

By recalling the aftermaths?
Kites gone down in tatters,
Kites fraying like flotsam
From the tops of the trees.

NESTS

1. Art Installation, Regent Square

The next day they were all in place,
Mounted and out-of-context:
Six cup nests of songbirds,
Each centered within a Lucite box

Cinched halfway up its tree.
And stretched beneath each nest,
A bar like a level, balancing
Dish-shaped feeders at either end.

The whole art spoke precision
Like that of Joseph Cornell,
Or the cases of wing-pinned insects
On display in the museum.

A world of thatch and plastic,
Carefully composed.
But beyond the cooped baskets
Is where the green limbs rose.

2. Gradeschool Exhibit, Carnegie Library

Pipe cleaners and paper
And raddled twigs—the grebe's nest
Floats on its shelf
As though woven to the waters

Its maker felt lapping about it,
Afternoons in the classroom,
Plaiting sea-green confetti
And pliant strands

Into make-shift weeds and grasses,
Hooping the first horizon
The nestlings would know.
A fourth-grade project

In habitable forms, the way
They fashion the world
As we go, learning
The various grammars for home.

THE BOOK OF THE DEAD

1. The Nestling

Already the ants are working their intricacies
Upon it, world without end.

They unburden the bones which were only
The barest of reeds to begin with,

They rinse themselves in the light
And hurry on. There is no mystery for them

In the unfinished body with its gummed wings
And few feathers and dangling limp feet.

The bird is simply another thermal of the source
They spend themselves uncovering.

And I, who am loathe to hold it in my hands,
What right have I to quarrel

With any of heaven's precise, cold terms?
Or any of the earth's?

2. Waking at Night

All night I tossed fitfully as one whose sleep
Was a passage to the same bad dream
That set my flesh crawling, the smallest motes
Of moonlight falling through the screen,

And then beyond it to where my father lay
As evening filled his room, the faint ants spilled
In endless waves out across the ceiling.

Figments of his shadows, he watched them
Swarm from the curtains, the seams of light
In the blinds, pouring upside-down around him,
Covering his sheets like wrinkles he kept trying
To smooth. Nor could anything but sleep
Soothe him, no matter what measures we used
To chase the small hoards from his sight.

Now, tossing awake all night, the pale motes
Of moonlight sifting about me
As if littering my sleep, I kick loose the covers
To see if my sheets are swarming for real,
Or whether I've only been dreaming again
Of my father, whose room grew dark
That evening when bits of the night came in.

3. Walton Hall of Ancient Egypt, Carnegie Museum

Feted and caulked, wound with strips
Of swaddling, the blunt Egyptian body
Lies bundled in its stiff shreds as in mache,

As though death might be finessed
The way life was not, and this vessel
Drifting on the waters of the dead—

A trenched bed eddying into your sight.
And in the display case beyond it:
The inlaid lid of a coffin blooming

With spectral flowers, the hawk-faced god
Fired in clay, and the chiseled *ankh*,
And the dry, meticulous veins . . .

Everything but the gold the great ants roll
From the underworld, the scarab beetle
That pushes up the disk of the sun.

SUMMER SONGS

1. Lawn Umbrella

A kind of sundial, with its wafer's worth
Of shade ellipsed on the ground around it.
The green faceted canvas. That dreidel
Of sprockets and wooden spokes, festive

As a pennant planted on a pole. Or stemmed
In the vase of the ornate cast-iron base.
Pinioned, it seems, like one of the wings
Leonardo drew, dreaming of such things.

2. House Deck

Like the family in the tree, we're up here
Summers, the night sky focusing its lights.
Deneb first and the Dippers, the north star
Pole-point to that chart. Closer at hand,

At eye-level in the invisible, the soft coals
Of fireflies drift upward from the lawn,
And with them, the dim swaddling moths.
The silk trees feathery with blossom.

SPIRIT IN THE DARK

What to make of the night we sat up late,
Listening to Beethoven's *Ninth*

In that otherwise darkened apartment?
The New York Philharmonic

Was gathering together the fragments
At the fourth movement's start—

Momentum they'd ride like a wave
Through the fanfare and final chorus—

When we felt something else enter the air,
A front in the weather of the room.

It sat us upright on the edge of our chairs
While it tracked toward the record

And hung suspended for a measure or two
Above the still point of the stylus.

Then, just as steadily, it withdrew,
A patch of fog that had been burned off . . .

The look the dead raised on your face
Must have been the same on my own.

"What was that?" our expressions asked.
Decades later, I'd still like to know.

And what changes, if any, were played
Upon us? And did any of them take?

"Be embraced," the chorus sang,
And then the crescendo and kettledrums,

The whole *Ninth* welling before us
Before fading as well from the room.

THIS SIDE OF HIS WATERS:
A PRAYER FOR MY INFANT SON

for Andrew

The underwater blue of moonlight
Bathing their tessellated shapes,

I lay dreaming of hawksbill hatchlings
Returning to the sea,

And had spied one struggling
Among the foam-laced waves

When that wail began to surface through me:
Not the familiar summons for milk,

But terror bursting darkly through the house,
Smearing its pulp on our walls.

And yet when we rushed into the nursery
There was nothing but the baby,

Still crying in his sleep,
The moon in the window above him.

A medusa rising on the waters of the night,
Did it flood his slumbers with fright?

Reaching down into the shadows,
The milk-filled crib of his breath,

I rocked my son on this side of his waters,
Easing him back upon the boat of sleep

I prayed would this time keep him
Lifted safely above the flood.

THE PITTSBURGH ZOO & AQUARIUM

1. Moon Jellyfish

The eclipse I once watched through an X-ray
Looked something like this darkness
In which they drift, trawling the currents for prey,
Their bodies' veils pulsing. Undulant
Hems, they'd wad out of water and decay,

But here in the night tides they rise and fall
And slide along the face of the reef
Without snagging—gauze and gossamer and caul—
Whole shoals of the other whose garments
Are light, being little moons after all.

2. Turtles

Rubblework and bedrock,
The pillared shells drift across
This quadrant of sunlight
And dust in which heat is still

Murderous at four o'clock.
For hours now we've made
Our slow way through the zoo's
Sour tenements, past

The torpor of great cats, bears
Pole-axed by August.
Past each replicated landscape
We descended the stair

To stand watching turtles
Ferry their plates above
The salt tides of the blood—
Shells rifted and scarred

As if by glaciers, the soft parts
Of the mosaic pebbling their skin.
They seemed to me again
To have simply been uncovered:

Cobbles of the living rock
Left by those waters,
Their massed hearts, tidal,
Burning on the sands.

3. *"Aquarium Reports Shark Deaths"*

Here's darkness to appall. Bonnetheads
And blacktips at the bottom of the tank,
Louvered gills gone slack, and the sleek
Relentless orbiting: hulks in a dead
Planetarium, the ozone-laced waters of its sky.
Grown perfect by the Pleistocene,
These have prowled with their spring-
Clipped teeth and wide outstaring eyes,
The harsh scales nerved like dentifrice.
When the heavens were clockwork
They turned on the carriage of the shaft—
Submerged millennia before us—
And here have come to rest, extinguished
Flames, guttered the length of the wick.

4. Octopus

Knobbed and small and tangled
In a corner of the tank,

It stares back at us with an eye
Like a bird's inside the massy sac.

And a bird's beak too, tucked up
In the midden about which it furls:

A cluster of sea-grapes bobbing
Among the softly nodding stalks.

And this teenaged girl beside us,
Tattooed and pierced,

Squawking "how gross!" so loudly
Even her boyfriend squirms,

What in all that amplitude
Of unhulled flesh so upsets her?

The octopus, for its part,
Neither pales with fright

Nor breaks out in those splotches
Dark as birthmarks—

The almost sexual rash it exhibits
When excited and sighting food.

5. Otters

Unlike water they flow uphill,
Out of water to the ledges
On the rocks, from where they spill
Downwards, convection's

Acrobats, moiling spouts
That slip the knots
In which they tie themselves, pelts
Sleeked back from the flat

Eager foreheads, the clean-
Lined, long-necked plunge,
Unencumbered by anything
That keeps them from

Their tireless, flat-out fun.
Even asleep they're crammed full
Of themselves. Awakened,
They're the glad heart of the pool

That proxies here as home.
What must it be like,
I wonder, to never once be lonely
Or burdened by the mind?

THE PRODIGAL'S VERSION OF EMSWORTH

for my cousin, Richard Beitel

Alone in bed in Mother's house, waiting for sleep,
I watch that tree in my window gleam
With the same cold fire of starlight
I dreamt of entering as a boy, scrambling down
The branches. Beyond it, the arbor,
The alley lined with fences and those garages
Like tenement flats, are still the same as well—
Though divorced at sixty and home for good,
My life feels like something I've remembered
From a dream. Here for the holidays,
My wife sleeping quietly beside me,
I'd feel the familiar weight of darkness
Take my shape, that scent like time in my nostrils.
Some of those nights, lying awake, I'd finally
Descend the stairs to stand in the shadowy rooms,
My eyes filling with whatever light
Came spilling through the blinds,
Though even in the dark I knew the whereabouts
Of each thing there, the way I could see my life:
Wife, children, the Connecticut house . . .

Here, this morning, I trimmed the hedge
My father planted, shearing its boxed shape
Out of the tangle it had lapsed into.
I weeded Mother's tomatoes—the patch I've dug
In the corner of the yard that catches most
Of the afternoon sun. I'd thought a man lay down
Each night and rose each morning
And his life lay there before him, clear as water
In a bowl. You could sink your hands into it.

You could cup it upwards to your face
And what poured through your fingers
Was spill-off and plenty, like grace.
Tonight, after supper, Mother and I sat out back
In that strange amber light you sometimes find
Before a storm, the sky gone gray above us,
The air tropic and saturate in the nap of the lawn.
Listening for the familiar sound of rain in the trees,
It struck me just how readily the familiar
Can change into something strange,
And I thought out loud, just how can that be?

REQUIEM FOR THE TREES

1. Blow Down

Thunderstorms the other night with wind shears
And lightning: one pure braid of current

And then another—that absolute carbide
Running to earth, slamming the circuit-breakers.

Two trees around the corner toppled across the wires,
Sparks showering the branches.

Trees in the park as well uprooted in a swath,
Leaves already wicking off the sap.

I climbed among them this morning, stunned
As always by the scale of that stillness,

The century's worth of time ticking from them
Like distances through which the vast herds fell.

One great unearthed wheel loomed before me,
Seven, eight feet high—

Clumps of dirt in the root-hairs, wattle-and-daub
From which the popped cords hung—

The whole ball strangely glowing, as if the light
Were something immanent and still abiding there.

2. Dutch Elm

My neighbor's been at it again today,
Rappelling among the branches of the blighted tree,

Rigging a block-and-tackle above where
His chainsaw passes, the huge sky streaming through.

Even leafless, even the sand-blasted gray of driftwood,
It's stood sentry in our alleyway.

Now, with the ends of the limbs lopped off,
It looks like a patient after the first surgeries,

The sky like afterwards with the alcohol and gauze.
Busy, he is happy, having found his way to mastery,

Managing the blight, the loss of all that greenery
Into the usable thermals of wood.

He reminds me of those settlers, circa 1850,
Climbing the masts of Indiana's last bur oaks,

Trying to sight the ends of the emptiness
To which they'd just come,

And failing that, plunging onward with their hymns,
Wreckage trailing behind them.

II

BLUES IN AUGUST

for Jimmy Muto

Thinking *the bright scarves of the cries*
Of children at play, I look out my window
And see the dark-haired boy there
With my sons, belly thrust before him,

His arms bent up at the elbows like small
Useless wings. A dangling thing,
He's seemed to me since learning
About his illness: the sudden collapses

And trouble with stairs, the halt muscles
Giving way. He doesn't know
This is final, like the light growing less
Each day, the summer almost over,

And screams at his mother that he's not
Going home, he wants to stay here
And play, leave him alone.
She holds him as though a gust of wind

Were ruffling her skirt, smoothing
His arms back down until he slackens
In that tangle and allows her to lead him off.
Just yesterday she was telling us about

The miraculous promise of the telethon,
"Our best hope now is Jerry Lewis,"
And I thought of how the dice toss
I believe in couldn't comfort anyone.

Lost momentarily from the rhythms,
My sons wander slowly back toward
Their games, leaving me alone
To puzzle the grief of things in August,

That weight sunk down inside its skins—
How the lank sap empties from the roots
And rot lavishes the ripeness,
And how long a diminishing the end obtains.

THE ICARUS OF FRICK PARK

The park at the end of summer:
Dogs and joggers, the yellow coltsfoot giving way
To the stained glass of the trees.

Only two days after the murder
And we're back to our routines. Still, had I walked
As usual the other day,

They'd have sped right past me,
Sluing the curves up Lancaster in a low white hurtling car.
I'd have cursed the gears and tires

Long before I reached Falls Ravine Trail
And that shape I'd have mistaken for trash bags
Before it turned into leaves,

Clothing, a body like a black hole
Contracting the field of light . . . Then fear alone
Would have seized me,

There in the marrow of the dying year.
Say I'd been drawn to his stillness just the same,
Close enough to mourn

The dark blood seeping into earth
And the earth that all too soon would be only
Another bare stretch of dirt.

I stand here where they found him,
Seeing how little of the world his death has disturbed,
The yellow tape down already,

And murmur words from Auden
For my prayer: *some untidy spot / Where the dogs go on*.
Then I'm gone as well:

Up the trail to where this summer
I'd pause to watch the white-clad seniors bowling—
Chucked balls following one another

Out across the expanse of lawn,
As though the planets were being rolled
In their slow and orderly courses.

GINKGOS

Maidenhairs and ancients,
    They branch along both sides
        Of Schenley Drive, bark
Deeply fissured, their leaves—

Fan-shaped and falling all week
    With the steady autumn rains—
        Plied upon the sidewalks.
PA KUO, the Chinese call them,

Duck's foot, noting resemblances.
    A dirty tree, my stepmother
        Would have replied, sick
With the fierce sexual reek

Of the ovaries, overly ripe
    And swollen and underfoot.
        Nor would she be comforted
In knowing these same leaves

Are found in coal seams
    Laid down millions of years ago:
        A black, bituminous mulch
Slowly composted into fossil.

I could tell her how today
    The gingkoes glistened within
        The mists of traffic as against
The background on a scroll,

Mention the women I passed
 Who were filling baskets
  With the bamboo-colored fruit.
We could talk of temple gardens,

Whole winter melon pond soup.
 Since when do you like Chinese
  Food? I can hear her scoff.
Who wants to rake those leaves?

Then I'd explain how pollens
 Drift from tree to tree, winds
  Showering the catkins out
In a sperm of small gold flowers.

WINDFALLS

1. *Late Night Listening to* The Band

A flock of finches, glinting gold,
Billows from the hedge-row,

The thin cold light of autumn
Returning evening to the earth.

I watched it for the first time
Years ago, a sky the drained gray

Of feathers left matted in a nest,
And heard it in that music

Like burnished wood: the brown
Album I've been playing since,

Its riffs on down the rhythms
To "King Harvest (Has Surely Come)."

Today even our twisting roads
Seemed to promise something more

Than the same play of landscape.
Even the dogwood in my yard,

Stiff leaves withered with flame,
Seemed a struck chord branching in air.

This evening, I sit listening
Once again to a music part foothill,

Part Bluebird blues, mournful
As the distances it empties into.

Later tonight, drunk on moonlight
And the pap of fermenting apples,

The raccoon will hear that muffled
Stomp rocking from the house,

telling us our hard times
are about to end,

Feel the windfall in his belly
Burning hot and raucous as song.

2. *The Afternoon of the Faun*

Smoke, and then the slender rain-
Filled trees they have stepped lightly
Among—up from the hollow

Where October's full-blown still
In its thatch of leaf and shadow—
The three deer stare back at me

Before continuing their browse
Across the slope of the field, toward
Frew Avenue and the back campus.

I watch them lower their faces
As if to drink from the surface
Of the earth, then sniff the air

For windfalls: their alert still forms
      More surprising than ever, here
            In the heart of Pittsburgh!

Last night at the reading I listened
      As someone described those first squat
            Atomic bombs as being *pure body*,

Even though, like the mind, they render
      The world abstract. Even though
            They drift like wood-smoke,

Shimmering in a thicket of the senses,
      I've seen deer dressed down
            To the dark of the carcass,

Hacked shins stacked like kindling
      Among scent glands and slops.
            Years ago, on another campus,

I watched a big hawk rip into a blue jay
      There in the center of the quad,
            While just as here, students passed

Distractedly around it. When the hawk
      Looked up at me, it was like staring
            Into matter being hammered out—

A furnace where even stones would burn,
      Dense and russet as apples
            Among which the shy deer browse.

THE NEST

i.

Unlike the windfall of shucked skins and antlers
I've brought back over the years,
I unpack the nest from a bag I'd left in the attic,
Careful to avoid the wreathed thorns bristling around it,
Amazed once more by the intricate whorls,
The way it's been woven out of the available world.

ii.

I found it in the leaves one day, fallen but still intact,
And remember taking note of the craft,
As I do now—the delicate thatch that swirls
From the smallest twigs outward—and how, furled
Among the down, was a lock of hair my wife had flung
Onto the lawn, that quiet summer, barbering our sons.

KEEPSAKES: A POCKET GUIDE
TO THE MEMORABILIA IN THE ROOM

1. My Father-in-Law's Cigar Case

A snug and perfect, breast-pocket fit,
The glove leather's tucked in grooves
For three cigars to slip into like fingers,
The tanned pebbly grain darkened

With the gift of his oils. And the scent
Of tobacco! Great leaves curing in shafts
Of light, brown and biscuit and sorrel,
The rolled smoke waiting as if housed

Inside a bough. Strange how we seem
To saturate the things we leave behind,
Which our lives in passing have touched.
How, like our lives, they are gathered up.

2. "Early Jazz Greats" Trading Cards
by R. Crumb

These, even though commissioned,
Came clearly from the heart. Remember
In *Crumb* how he sat in his living room,
Listening in the dark to the music?

"One of the few times," he explained,
"I actually have a kind of love for humanity."
I slip them from the box—"Fatha" Hines
And Satchmo and a beaming Sidney Bechet—

Portraits in a pocket-sized Uffizi,
Face up and played in order before me.
How deftly they've been posed
Beside their instruments, cameoed

As if on the flaps of a carnival tent.
The deck's merely a convention, like melody,
There being too few musicians in it
To reprise a single combo,

Let alone trade—unless, that is,
You wanted to swap the entire boxed set.
But what would be the sense of that?
In it, they're having the time of their lives.

3. Change Purse

A crumpled pocket of clasped black leather
The size and shape of a dried plum,
My grandfather had it with him
When he fell in the mills, back out of time.

It's filled with the eight coins he was carrying:
A dollar-twelve's worth of loose change.
Not even the value of the metals
For which the pay-dirt body can be exchanged.

I pay them out again, the Indian-head pennies
And Liberty dimes, studying wreaths and faces,
The turn-of-the-century's cusps of dates,
Still actuarial, still trying to square accounts.

4. Letter Opener

More curio than memento, this ornate blade,
Flat and handleless, the caravan of elephants
Along its spine like knots of a macramé.

I'm glad it's actually plastic and not the sliver
Of tusk it's been made to resemble—a shiv
Of hand-carved ivory pocketed during the Raj.

5. Pocket Watches

Three small gleaming glass and metal suns
Passed down in the family,
Each with its circumference of numbers,
The inset, second hand orbit
At the bottom of each face.

5:26, 6:50, 1:05. One side of the meridian
Or the other. Either way
Each is an instance of something stopped,
Though I've tried coaxing moments from them,
Rocking the balance cocks and wheels.

Unfastening the backs, you can see
All the racks, levers, springs, and gears
That once worked together so perfectly.
All forms, I remember, hold energy
against the flow of time.

"GONNA DIE WITH MY HAMMER IN MY HAND"

Anthology of American Folk Music

I heard it first during the folk revival,
    The Williamson Brothers and Curry
        With their version of "John Henry,"

                                          .

That high ethyl edge to their voices
    Where the notes frayed off into time,
        The failure of the early acetates

To fully capture the music they miked.
    Whatever the title, *steel drivin' man*
        Is the phrase that told me, growing up,

That he was one of our own.
    Steel was coal raised up, I'd thought,
        Or broken back down, something

You turned into song. A river below us
    The ferrous of rust. A city that rose
        From a scrap pile. Those nights

I'd lie awake listening to the trains
    In Homestead and the way they dopplered
        Back against their passage,

Billowing the distances with sound.
    Monday morning on the Eastbound train . . .
        I'd range along both sets of tracks

After school, kicking up bent spikes,
    The glisters fallen off the coal cars,
        Any of the rubble lying hedged in place

Between the creosote-soaked ties.
    Down there at ear-level I could hear it—
        That first faint freight-train popping

Like a knife on a slide guitar,
    Sparks struck the length of the track bed
        till the hammer caught on fire.

III

sheet music

1. THE MODERN JAZZ QUARTET IN CONCERT: CARNEGIE MUSIC HALL, PITTSBURGH, 1964

Trompe l'oeil of the instruments set on stage,
The bass upright and glowing like rose-
Wood, like a vase in which flowers were scrolled.
Brass bloom of the high hat. The Steinway
Limpid in lacquer. And now the Quartet, formal
As their music which begins, legato,
Reverberating through the Hall: "Django,"
Let's say, the slow measured gait of its cortege.

And now the first notes spilling from the vibes until
The whole ensemble's shimmering precisely
About the beat, the music finds that stately
Weave with which it might carry us all
From march to strut to mortal frolic, cakewalking
Our little way in the huge and acoustic dark.

2. A LATE ELEGY FOR THELONIOUS MONK

1. *Straight, No Chaser*

He's on stage, arms outstretched:
    A capped black dervish turning in space
As though through a falling snow,
        The dumb show of the flakes.

As though somehow that name,
    Sphere, occasioned its fulfillment.
Even here they're a little scary,
        Those lurching orbits, even if

No one seems to pay them any mind,
    Charlie Rouse descending the scales
Of his solo, the rest of the quartet—
        Ben Riley and Larry Gales—

Laying down the groove. Later
    In the movie, we'll see him spinning
In kitchens and hallways, airports and aisles.
        But what at the beginning

Seemed a kind of scuffled exuberance
    And waltz through the crowded world
Now looks like loss of balance.
        Vertiginous, really, this inward

Turning among scattered notes
    And dancing shifts of rhythm, this
Collapsing into silence
        And the coma's final eclipse.

2. High E in the Wind

Again this morning a cold rain's been pelting
The bare limbs filled with birds:

Dozens of them on each tree on our block,
Flocking like clustered notes. They happen

At once, and then are particular wet shapes,
Ruffling or still, or slowly rising, dragging

Their crusted knuckles across the slant wash
Of light they wake in, in which housewives

Stand at windows, half-dressed and dreaming
Of the rhythms they've moved to, in time.

Years ago we saw him standing between sets
Outside of the Village Vanguard. It seemed

He was listening to scraps of music
As they played among the half-lit streets.

And can't you hear it, even now—the first faint
Stridings of *Solitude, Blackbird, Body and Soul*

Drifting above the dark machinery of rivers
And bridges humming High E in the wind?

3. AT THE ROLLINS CONCERT

Point State Park, Pittsburgh

Sunday evening, festival's end, the light
Beginning to level along the Ohio

And reside, mid-register, on the flood plain
Of the park, the arc lamps and concert stage

They're readying for the last set,
Music unspooling from the tape deck.

Down here: blankets and backpacks, the ubiquitous
Frisbees disking the air, and behind us

A mother and her retarded child, head lolling,
Distracted by the crowd. And now Rollins,

Stepping out, flinging his tenor skyward as he rips
Into the opening chorus of "St. Thomas"—

A rooster flapping with the morning sun,
Harbor and market, rhythms bright as rum . . .

Which is when, behind us, the lost boy
Starts to moan, softly at first as a voice

In sleep, or sleep's own troubled murmurs.
Then, growing louder,

And seemingly pitched to some infinite woe,
Comes the wrenched, misshapen solo.

4. SOLOING

That was a bad time, let me tell you.
 I was taking Valium and there were
  Lawnmowers everywhere.

We'd been listening to Chet Baker
 And early Brubeck—those red, see-through
  Fantasy LPs in which the notes

Seemed pressed in pectin. My friend said
 It took him by surprise, meaning the divorce,
  His wife having taken up

With what he called *the brown rice*
 And cocaine crowd, leaving him
  To muddle as best as he could

Into his own ritual sense of separation.
 For her it was a kind of makeover:
  New clothes and furniture

And redecorating every corner of the house.
 That was when she taunted him:
  "Now I won't have to listen anymore

To that horrible music of yours,"
 And packing his records it occurred to him
  He'd never argue with her again.

So there was that, at least, to build on,
 And the boast that she'd been voting
  Republican all along, and the frilly

Heart-shaped pillow she'd just bought
For her nightstand. In the meantime,
He told me, he'd have to bear

The memory of those afternoons
They first made love after work,
The plum tree blooming in the window,

Late sun upon them as she'd start to quake,
And that trumpet aching
From the other room.

5. PRAISING THE BASS CLARINET

for James Carter and David Murray

i.

The full, round, bottom-belling sound
Of that bored tube of hardwood.
More blackthorn than licorice stick,
The keys a kind of piping
Like beamed notes and octaves
Gleaming the length of the staff.
The reed and pads and finger holes.
The satiny pitch to its finish.

ii.

Breathy, chthonic, a didgeridoo
Made to blossom in flowering roots,
Or in the right hands rumble
With the most wistful-sounding thunder.
Double down, it says, and *bottoms up*,
And *keep an ear to the ground*.

6. THE SORCERER'S APPRENTICE

Friday evening, music from the slung shelf
Of the console—LPs and those old plate-like 78s—
While in the antic kitchen my father sways
Beneath the dancehall light he pretends
Is on the ceiling. Performing sleights of hand,
He pours me a shot of Rolling Rock
From his own foaming bottle, a glass that fits
My grip, monkeys tumbling head-to-tail
Around it. And now another record drops
From the changer as if by magic. Magic too
Are the names, *Ben Webster* and *Lester Young*,
And the way that even blindfolded, he tells me,
He'd know whoever it was that's playing.

Now he amazes me with the loop of string
That slips through his fingers. And now
He palms a penny from behind my stepmother's
Startled ear, deposits it in my pocket,
And cracks open another beer. But she still feels
That conjured coin and will not believe it's gone,
Will not believe he is magical this evening
And beyond deceit. Silent while the record fades
From Sweet Lorraine to Georgia Brown,
We watch her rummage through her hair,
Its dry tindery nest, furious at us, frantic to find
That one red cent which is there no longer
And yet which lingers and, lingering, burns.

7. SONG FOR MY FATHER

He even looked a good deal like Goodman,
Especially when he was young—
The thinning hair and horned rims,

The same embouchure supplying his smile.
I like to picture him those evenings,
Boothed as usual in the Crawford Grill

While the din of voices gathered
Like instruments being tuned. And then,
Out of that rich antiphonal clamor,

How Deep Is the Ocean or *Honeysuckle Rose*,
Trellises of smoke in the spotlights,
The tenor's husky arpeggios . . .

*

Years later, when he seemed to be sleeping
In his chair, I hope he was listening instead.
On those walks, I want him out playing

With the hosts of the air, charting rhythms
With Erroll Garner on Orchid Street,
Comping on Scotia behind Dakota Staton.

And West Run Road, the creek in its froth
Of spill-off, graffiti fading like spume
On the stones—there'd be a favorite swatch

Of Strayhorn there: *Take the "A" Train,*
Or *Drawing Room Blues,* whose riffs
He'd bring back home, his own refrain.

8. "TURNPIKE": AN ELEGY FOR CLIFFORD BROWN ON THE ANNIVERSARY OF HIS DEATH

i.

Velocity. Even on the alternate take
He comes in on all cylinders, the valves
Of the trumpet smooth and lubed:

Triplets and those eighths he favored
Storming out. I think of him that night
In Philadelphia, finishing the last set,

Then hitting the turnpike right away
For a gig in Ohio, though actually
Ritchie Powell's wife did the driving.

ii.

Actually, in the rarified air of the studios
At WOR, it's still 1953, three years
Before the car crash that killed them.

Brownie's lilt and urgency here is all
Arrival, phrases effortlessly spun out.
And why not? He's not going anywhere.

It's spring in Manhattan, the trees in bloom.
They've still to cut "Get Happy"
And "It Could Happen to You."

9. LISTENING TO BUD POWELL'S *PARISIAN THOROUGHFARES* (SESSIONS FROM 1957-1961): A PALIMPSEST FOR WILLIAM MATTHEWS

It's Paris, digitally formatted,
      And behind the clatter of silverware
And Kenny Clarke's prodding of time—

The murmurous wash of table talk,
      Powell's own moaning vamps—
Flash those snatches of intermittent fire

He can still sometimes manage.
      In 1959, when Matthews caught him,
The pianist's right hand kept foundering

Among its runs and Bill imagined pain
      As a kind of dull accompaniment
A whole life could get swamped by.

If not for the year, he could have been
      Listening to "Yesterdays"
(Club Saint-Germain, 1957) and Powell

Shouting out *B minor!* as if things
      Weren't funereal enough. I'm trying
To remember which cassette of his

I happened to have in the truck
      The evening Bill and I hurried back
From the bar in time for his reading.

That was when, 1989? A late spring
        In the Poconos, the polite applause
Of students at the end of his lines.

Then afterwards, dinner with the fawning
        Faculty, all background noise.
Caught in the analog transfer from the old

Mythic Sound LPs, he could be part
        Of the background I'm hearing now,
Ordering his second scotch at either

The Blue Note or Saint-Germain.
        In 1997, I first heard of his death
From a woman walking down a flight

Of stairs, and have imagined it ever since
        As a kind of descending figure
Visited upon the music like a minor key.

10. MINGUS MEETS THE UNKNOWN
IN THE PERSON OF HORACE PARLAN

Pittsburgh, 1956

A late night jam and the growling Mingus
Is head down, stropping the strings,
Trying to cut this unknown pianist,
A local kid, whose left hand's blistering
The keyboard: single-note solos and chords
And, behind them, something of that old
Abyssinian mournfulness and splendor
Mingus uses in "Better Git Hit in Yo Soul."

Tonight, because he's all ears, or because
The pitch of his own playing absorbs him,
Hunched in the tonic and after-hours' light,
He never notices Horace Parlan's stricken
Right hand skimming among the octaves,
Inflections the polio can't get to, or blight.

IV

THE WEATHER IN DECEMBER

1. Deer in Rain, New Homestead Hill

Umber and gray, in the welter of the thicket,
Wet light streaking the trees,
In the stillness of the dream they inhabit,
Four deer forage among the fallen leaves,
White tails flashing, undergrowth now gone
From the half-lit rooms. The Chinese Elm
They slept beneath, our summer lawn,
Are numb and blasted. The does gun-metal,
Fawns having begun to lose the spoor-
Colored markings tracking their backs.
Black roots and ink-caps. So much gradual
Darkness to this world! And now my Aunt Martha,
Dead in Wexford in a nursing home,
Her stark body cold as the stars.

2. Manger and Trees, Carnegie Museum

In the story of the baby who saves the world
By being born into it—as though the body
Were the spirit's rind and not its root and seed—
These figure in widening circles:
Wise men and shepherds, the stable beasts,
Angels in clouds of drapery
Kettling above the crowded streets,
The carefully painted faces. Pageantry
Like a model train's. And beyond it

The dark flames of the evergreens: a forest
In the room. They tower above me even now,
The wintry boughs, that scale out of childhood,
The deep oils spiring and the burning crowns,
Out of the stalled star and the heartwood.

MARTHA AT THE THRESHOLD OF HEAVEN

Martha Beitel, 1901-1997

I knew it was down there,
Having descended one evening
Into a cellar filled with shadows
Flung skittering from the bulb,

And made my way back hurriedly
To the surface of my rooms,
Wondering what crack it found
To follow its thin song through.

That night I dreamt of ripe fruit
Dropping from trees, the air
Grown mazy with their flight.
The wet snouts, and the teeth.

Descending again in the morning,
The bat was nowhere to be seen.
Nor, in the weeks into winter,
Did it startle me again

Till the Whirlpool filled with water
And a screeching like enamel's
Being scraped. All the same,
What I managed to lift

From the washer was hardly
The death's-head of my dream.
A sodden little body was all
I found, a sopping fetish

Of twigs and leaves. I carried it,
Dripping, up the cellar steps
And tossed it out onto the snow.
And there it remained for days,

Worn through at the shoulders
Like something needing mending.
Something small and fallen
I've tried ever since to place.

BLUES FOR THE YOUNG WOMAN
FROZEN TO DEATH WHILE MAKING
THE SHAPES OF ANGELS IN THE SNOW

Drunk, I would guess, and defenseless
Against even the familiar shopworn forms
Beauty loves to take on, and longing,

She sat alone, the night after Christmas,
Staring down into the darkness next door
Where the ground was an eidering

Of snow, foot-thick now and griseous—
A field into which she might fall short
Of flight, then clamber up again, fledgling

And naked except for the nightdress
In which she'll come to light, like morning,
Among the banked and staggered wings.

JUNCO

i.

Slate to dusk to snow, like the sky
Against the winter roofs, the junco
Lights below the feeder, out of the wind,

In the copse of shelter the crab apples
Make, untrimmed beside the porch.
Monochrome and charcoal, the white

Of the belly looks almost lit, almost
Immaculate as a sheet of vellum
Nothing's been permitted to touch—

Not even the city air, or the smoke
From chimneys down-drafting in gusts.
Not even the snow's less smudged.

Beyond the trees I can see the dark
Thatch of hedges bordering the alley,
The black vines climbing a garden wall.

ii.

Even Audubon glimpsed them in winter,
But south, on the sprigs of a cotton-gum,
Dark fruit tasseled and out of season,

The background blank as snow,
Though tinted so the white of the belly
Stands out. And yet even Audubon

Has not caught how fully the slate
Feathers blot up light, softly as lamp-black,
The slender chimney's plume of ash.

The scale seems slight. Or perhaps
It's the lack of winter in the scale
Of light as it flurries into evening

All afternoon, that one dull arc-lamp
Burning in the alley, the shadow
Of the bird below it, darkening the snow.

BEAKMAN'S BACTERIA FARM

Petri, we read, invented these flat lidded dishes
In order to culture creatures
Teeming as angels on the head of a pin.

We're to fill them each with gelatin,
Swabbed with germs from ears and noses,
The numinous bacteria of the air.

Tiny animalcules, Leeuwenhoek called them,
Peering into his Holland of pond water,
Feeling the foundations shift.

In the ground glass and optics of the 17th century
They even thought of cells as compartments,
Small rooms latticed as combs,

The light of that world clear and steady
Wherever it happened to flow.
Here, if Beakman's any guide,

We're harboring monsters from a TV show,
Viruses like ants queuing to a picnic.
It won't be long before we're viewing

The disked profusion of microbes
Through the lenses of a microscope:
My wife, my sons, immersed

In the stippled blooming of a world
That's magical as pollination's,
Or those maps in Dutch paintings

Rendered in the recessed rooms
We're offered the barest glimpse of,
The known world there in miniature.

DIPTYCH: STILL LIFE & MEMORY

1. *Trophy of the Hunt* (1885),
   Carnegie Museum of Art

> The world was once real, imagine. Rabbit,
> Cord, nail, palpable as the pigments in paint,
> The rust of blood dribbled on the door
> Of the canvas. You came up close and stared
> At a surface in which things were held:
> Bolts and boards, the actual in lavish detail.
>
> In the Gilded Age, from across the room,
> Light on the level in the painting, the way
> It falls in season on autumn afternoons,
> The way light pearls in the pelt of the rabbit
> Or lies along the scroll-like hinges, giving
> Them depth, all made museum galleries gasp.
>
> A world as stiff and stubborn as the one
> They were urged to endorse. Not the semblance
> But the thing, weight drawn taut on the cord.

2. *Small Game Season,* 1958,
   Emsworth, Pennsylvania

> Not the king of ghosts, but the poor flesh
> Battered and torn, that wintry Thanksgiving
> In Emsworth, laughter on the back stairs
> And my uncles suddenly loud in the kitchen,

Aunts complaining about the blood
Until the rabbits were slapped in the sink.

I watched them then, bleeding and raw,
The soft fur flecked with red and the gravel
Singes of shot: clouds gouged out of earth.
They'd just been swung before me, eye-level
And head down, as on an axis of the field,
Magnified like nothing else, and more real.

THE HOUSE ON INTERBORO AVENUE

1. *The Laundry Chute*

A built-in, trap-doored podium, it stood in the corner
Of my aunt's upstairs hallway, above the shaft
That plumbed the house and came out in the basement,

Bull's eye above the basket laundry dropped into.
A bucket down a well. Only this was lugged back up,
Folded and stacked, to be flung in a heap once more.

The day I hauled myself upon it and watched her
Sorting wash, two stories below me, marked
My first glimpse into the usual's surprising shifts.

As did her fright that I might spill from the ceiling
Like some quattrocento angel from a painted sky,
The motherless child who'd fallen already into her care.

2. *The Bath*

In a room of gleaming white enamel: the washbasin
Where I brushed my teeth, the candle-watted sconces
Above it and, underneath, that curved pelican gullet.

Still better was the tub, claw-footed and cast, massive
As one of the Elgin Marbles. I could stretch out in it
And sink, snug beneath the waters and lulling steam.

3. Pocket Doors

It seemed as though the whole wall hung on hinges
And disappeared. Its panels sheer as the sea's.
As though the room reemerged when they closed.

LOOKING AT PETER MILTON'S *COMPLETE PRINTS*,
1960–1996

Even in the prints of Peter Milton, where
Their solidity's only a surface depth,
I find the rows of Brownstones comforting,
And the elegant one-point perspective

By which he's set them clear of time.
Yet once inside, in the past's foyer,
I'd likely float ghostly as a day moon
On the landing at the top of the stair—

Like that face in *The Jolly Corner*
Gazing back at us from the upper part
Of an interior etched in crepe-black ink,
Mezzotint the tarnish of the plate.

In the first house we moved to
When I was a child, I'd look from the level
Of the landing on my way to bed,
Not yet haunted or haunting myself,

The firm world under my feet.
Now I see myself as in a dream, floating
Above the little, spot-lit stage
On which my parents are sitting.

That's either a vase in the Milton
Or hurricane lamp. In the train station gloom
It's hard to say, the vault of the wall
Behind it, etched lines cut into time.

Isn't that the ground from which we're lifted?
It still feels I'm leaning against what's not there.
In the etching the rail of the banister
Stops halfway up the stair.

CRUSOE IN HOMESTEAD

Estate of Joanne Carr to Toth Holdings Inc.,
328 E. 16ᵗʰ Ave., $20,000.
—PITTSBURGH POST-GAZETTE

All week I've been railing against Crusoe,
For whom home was a ghostly geography

More real than his own—his cave a Cellar,
Mortar a tortoise shell—and now

Here's mine in the real estate listings,
How many closings since we sold it

The summer I turned four? What's exile,
Anyway, but one of the forms of longing,

And what's a more permanent address?
"When I came to *England*," he tells us,

"I was as perfect a Stranger to all the World,
as if I had never been known there."

And in that England on Sixteenth Avenue,
Where not even the cellar

In which I once locked my stepmother
Is a treasure of hoarded time,

What would I be looking to get back to,
Or find, but a house as dull as the clouds,

The late century's worth of weather
It seems to be wearing whenever I happen by?

Nor inside, where most of my memories
Are hand-me-downs, am I likely to recognize

A thing—not the honeycombed gas grates
Or panes of glass rippling within their frames.

The bedroom in which my mother died,
The parlor where my grandfather lay in state

After dying in the mills, would only mirror
The light alone, *as if I had never been*

known there. And Crusoe? Near the end
Of his adventures, isolate and growing old,

He's haunted as always with the possible,
For whom departure is still the only home.

V

IN THE MUSEUM

1. Fossils: Carnegie Museum of Natural History

Bodies in a bas-relief, as though laminated
In limestone, the dragonflies slant
On their familiar stalks—
                             canted sticks of incense,
Their veined wings shaped like maple seeds.

I return again to their stillness,
                                    to shelved bodies
Held in cases lidded with light,
The ribbed fall of shadows on a wall.

I marvel at what shapes darkness takes,
Undisturbed in the drift of stone, at pale slabs
Clean as plaster in which the dust
Has been kept whole, pressed in rifted plates.

I come back to the ridged anatomies,
Embossments of chalk,
The slow mineral flowering of time into bone.

2. Diorama, Polar World: Wyckoff Hall of Arctic Life

In a white world whose shapes are cut
From tusk and soapstone, the breath-laden light,
A sort of *tableau vivant*:
                           the bone tip
Of this harpoon aimed inches above the ice,
Hasped with thong to the long shaft

And the hunter behind it, niched and Inuit,
Hardly more still than he'd be for real
Those endless hours at the blow-hole.

He's watching, it says, for the ascending seal
He'll haul among breaching waters
Out onto the floe—
                dead center of an eruption
Breaking against the wheeling gulls
And frenzy of the sled dogs, the risen body
Opened up and rummaged like the sea.

3. Dermestid Beetles: Section of Invertebrate Zoology

Moths mounted in columns under polished glass,
Bees frowzy in black honey,
Walled inside their vented hives.

While over here, in paired terrariums,
The resurrection of the body has already begun:
Bones stripped down to the remnant tufts
Of fur and jerky—
                unhinged sockets, ruddled cups—
All seething with those insects.

They'd devour the building if they could,
Unhousing larvae from the marrow.
They'd convey the world to light,
                      interns
Of the underlife, trephining their disks of bone.

Or spill across each other as if spawned by matter,
Their teeth the teeth of cogs.

TWO DEGREES EAST, THREE DEGREES WEST

1. Giacometti Sculptures, Carnegie Museum of Art

As if the light itself were caustic,
They stand against a wall in the museum,

His little battery of statues, bodies slim as cotter-pins,
While out on the floor beyond them,

A life-sized figure, clinkered and gaunt,
Strides as if from a furnace.

Here instead of endless talk are mute bodies
Pegged in place, men endlessly walking,

Though it's mark-time-march
On the bases on which they've been set.

That clinkered figure, for instance:
He could be a sinter or the charred shaft of a match,

A persistence launched upon the emptiness.
Which is his triumph, after all,

Naked and striding head-high toward the horizon
Which keeps receding before his feet.

2. Passing the Angels, Saw Mill Run Boulevard

In the blue wash of evening,
Where the highway climbs into the same hue of heaven—

The ridges wholly flattened
Into successive, fading, waves of mist—

I entered the stream of traffic, traveling east
Out of the sun, and found myself following

A battered little truck from whose bed rose shafts
Of metal: mirror-colored spires,

Polished as machinery fresh from the shop.
Sculpture, I thought, or some public ornamentation,

Minimalist and sleek,
And so pulled up alongside him to have a closer read.

Only then did I see how they held the light
Like weather against their stormy skins,

The wings as barbed as pike-staffs
And the faces flashing their welded alleluias.

MUSEUM PIECES

1. Aztec Calendar Stone

The Face of the Sun, concentric with orbits
And boxed glyphs worked into stone—
Twenty-four tons worth, trussed upright
In the center of the cloistered room
I'd just walked into when it stopped me cold,
Like hands checked flat against my chest.
My flesh was all attention, turned to the aura
The plume-headed planets threw off,
And the days, constellated in totems
Of Wind and Flower and Flint.
And then that pressure-chamber density
Increasing its hold all around me.
I was being siphoned into the centuries
Of saturated stone, or so it seemed,
On the brink of the marvelous, where
The rooms I'd stepped from ceased to exist,
And the rest of the city's polished levels.
A wheel on the rim of its heavens,
Basalt like gravity's black hole . . .
And then that sudden disruption
When my friend came bustling into the room,
Seeing nothing out of the ordinary
In which he'd just found me,
The current now gone from the stone.

2. *Peregrine Falcon Eggs, c. 1939*

A clutch of mottled granite or gray
Lapis lazuli eggs, nestled in cotton batting
As if in down, and planetary,
Though more the color of storm clouds.
You can see what Brancusi saw in that form—
His *Sculpture for the Blind*—
And wanted us to see as a kind of Braille,
Hands-on like a sculptor. These, though,
Being fragile and riddled with DDT,
Can't be touched or hatched. Intact instead,
They're massed in their carton as if composed
And lovely in spite of everything—
Flecked, smooth pebbles
Upon which the light falls like a breath.

3. *Specimens, Herbarium*

Arranged figure-and-ground on their pages,
They're the actual illustrations of themselves,
Pressed flat and paraphrased
In the paragraphs below them. And exact,
Down to the slightest detail—
As in this *small herb under oil palm, growing
from tuber*, its heart-shaped leaves
And flowers like wheals of blotted blood—
Half-a-million, all alphabetized,
Mounted in their matter-of-factness,
Tallies of the species, cut-and-dried.

WALNUT: FOUR SKETCHES

i.

>The great limbs branching, ply on ply,
>Sky to light to darker green like color on a chart,
>Its leaves flame-shaped, seven to a stalk,
>Flaring like metal at the ribs, the black shells
>Even now indelible in the memory.

ii.

>The summer that I tried to draw *nothing*,
>The shapes between the leaves,
>My page filled with its tree as though by default,
>Like a poem emerging line by line
>From nothing, syntax, the tree inside the air.

iii.

>"We buy standing timber," the card read,
>Tucked in our door—someone's offer
>To break it down into beams and board feet,
>Into natural resource, scaling ladders from which
>To stride into the canopy as if from the sky.

iv.

One whole school year I drew a family tree
As a favor for a teacher, each tier of limbs
Spiked with names, clear to the upperstory,
A family branching from bole to crown,
Traced on paper, flesh of the flesh of the tree.

THE DRAWING LESSON

Art Class, Robert Qualters,
Woodlawn Junior High School, 1960

Passing above the bowed heads of students
At their desks, I watch as hands try to follow
The contours of the fox I've set before them,

Lank and stuffed in the fluorescent air.
For years now the pelt, mangy with moths,
Has surrounded nothing that moves,

And now moves through nothing, front paw
Lifted in a tentative step. How unlike
That bristling red cursive Winslow Homer set

Leg-deep in snow, bounding beneath
The storming crows! The day burns slowly
Across our windows, pane by pane,

Like foxfire across a marsh. It's all angle
And incidence, I try to tell them, how the ears,
Though they dishevel slower than sight,

Are still fraying apart like cardboard
Or the frozen frame of a filmstrip bursting
Into light. All week long beyond us

The bare trees, Xerox-gray, have made a nave
Of the road. Now again today I stroll among
The quiet aisles, above the squinched studies,

Looking for lines alert with the quickness
Of fox—*small-boned, plumed, hanging fire*—
And come instead to see the ways in which

It's stepped free of itself, its rigged body,
Disappearing stealthily during the drawing
To someplace they won't even be able to trace.

"TIN ROOF BLUES"

i.

Winter: a two-block woodcut.
Black for the branches, gray for the gunmetal sky.
(For snow, the white ground of rice paper.)
The season of form, as one naturalist has it,
North enough to have noted such things,
The tassels on the ornamental grasses
Crested and stiff, and the thin sprung leaves
The phoebes once flitted among.

ii.

I listened to Sidney Bechet's "Tin Roof Blues"
On an afternoon like this, years ago,
And have thought ever since of the winter sky
As flat-seamed panels of a roof—
Its caulk and flashing and cloudy light—
Latticed and screwed down with the cold.

GHOST SONATA

they answer us with silence
—RILKE

This wasn't All Soul's Night,
Trees shimmering like live oaks in tissue wraiths,
The children in Day-Glo skeletons.

Nor the spirit's howling,
Barometric, in air. This was a kind of Uri Geller,
Manic, at work on matter,

Pulling the plugs on lamp cords,
Pitching pennies about the room. It even slipped
A teaspoon beneath our covers—

Stunts all part of the repertoire
Meant to chase us out of doors. The local word
For them was *poltergeist.*

Sprites of a minor havoc,
Their idea of a joke was to throw into you
Just this sort of fright.

I slipped a sheet of paper
In my typewriter, an improvised Ouija on which
The dead might float a note,

But nothing came of it.
Whole hours passed as we peered into shadows
For whatever might be next.

Which is when the crosses
Started to appear, scrawled on mirrors and walls,
Scratched into the enamel

On that one kitchen cabinet.
I thought of Revelation, *the Lamb slain from
the foundation of the world,*

And then of the ram's head
From a recent dream, severed, its whorled horns
Changed to wings.

What happened after that—
Snap of static, the windless stir of curtains—
Was mostly denouement.

I'm still not sure if we were
Being pranked or witnessing the rage of energy
To be housed once more.

Or why, at four A.M.,
Just like my wife predicted, the town dogs began
Their unearthly chorus—

A ghostly sonata that rose
From the backyards till dawn, when we stumbled
At last into our bed,

Serenaded by traffic
And the waking world. It took awhile, in the dusk
Of the rooms we woke in,

To sort through it again,
Checking drawers, packing the typewriter away.
Imagine our amazement

When, back in the kitchen,
We found the enamel on that cabinet unscratched,
Where just hours before

A cross had been
And something was now rescinded
Or restored.

ACKNOWLEDGMENTS

Arts & Letters: "In the Museum," "Walnut: Four Sketches," "Nests," "A Late Elegy for Thelonious Monk," "Diptych: Still Life & Memory."

Brilliant Corners: "The Sorcerer's Apprentice," "At the Rollins Concert," "Soloing," "Praising the Bass Clarinet," "Song for My Father," "Listening to Bud Powell's *Parisian Thoroughfares* (Sessions from 1957–1961): A Palimpsest for William Matthews," "'Tin Roof Blues.'"

Cincinnati Poetry Review: "This Side of His Waters."

Cumberland Poetry Review: "Kites."

Field: "Turtles," "Octopus."

Great River Review: "Summer Songs," "Ghost Sonata."

Green Mountain Review: "The Icarus of Frick Park."

The Laurel Review: "The Prodigal's Version of Emsworth," "The Modern Jazz Quartet in Concert: Carnegie Music Hall, Pittsburgh, 1964."

Manoa: "Late Night Listening to *The Band.*"

Midwest Poetry Review: "The Afternoon of the Faun."

The Missouri Review: "The Book of the Dead."

New Letters: "The Nest," "'Turnpike': An Elegy for Clifford Brown on the Anniversary of His Death."

North Atlantic Review: "Ginkgos," "Junco."

Notre Dame Review: "Moon Jellyfish," "'Aquarium Reports Shark Deaths,'" "Otters," "Keepsakes: A Pocket Guide to the Memorabilia in the Room."

Pittsburgh Post-Gazette: "Mingus Meets the Unknown in the Person of Horace Parlan."

Prairie Schooner: "Spirit in the Dark," "Requiem for the Trees," "'Gonna Die with My Hammer in My Hand,'" "Museum Pieces."

Quarterly West: "The Music Lesson."

The Southern Review: "Beakman's Bacteria Farm," "Blues in August," "The Weather in December," "Martha at the Threshold of Heaven," "Blues for the Young Woman Frozen to Death While Making the Shapes of Angels in the Snow," "Crusoe in Homestead."

Sou'wester: "Looking at Peter Milton's *Complete Prints, 1960–1996.*"

Washington Square: "The House on Interboro Avenue."

West Branch: "The Drawing Lesson."

The poems in "'Two Degrees East, Three Degrees West'" were published, respectively, in *The Southern Review* and *The Widener Review.*

"Kites" was reprinted in *Poetry Calendar* 2010, edited by Shafiq Naz, Alhambra Publishing.

I would also like to acknowledge a grant from the National Endowment for the Arts.

NOTES

"The Icarus of Frick Park": The lines in italics are from Auden's great meditation on the exclusive nature of suffering, *"Musee des Beaux Arts."*

"Keepsakes: A Pocket Guide to the Memorabilia in the Room": The sentence in italics, with which the poem concludes, is from William Irwin Thompson's *Evil and World Order.*

"At the Rollins Concert": "St. Thomas," a Rollins standard, refers to the capital of the Virgin Islands and not the religious figure.

"Listening to Bud Powell's *Parisian Thoroughfares* (Sessions from 1957–1961): A Palimpsest for William Matthews": The poem alludes to Matthews' "Bud Powell, Paris, 1959," which first appeared in his book *Rising and Falling.*

"The Weather in December": Each year during the holidays, in its Hall of Architecture, the Carnegie Museum exhibited a Neapolitan *Precipio* —a Nativity of carved figures and animals. Decorated Christmas trees were also installed in the Hall at this time.

"Diptych: Still Life & Memory": The painting *Trophy of the Hunt* is one of the *trompe l'oeils* of the American artist, William Harnett.

"Looking at Peter Milton's *Complete Prints, 1960-1996*": Milton executed two sequences of resist-ground etchings and engravings based on the James short story.

"Museum Pieces": Constantin Brancusi (1876-1957) was one of the last century's great sculptors, his *Sculpture for the Blind* (1916) an egg-shaped piece of marble, 10″ high, meant to be touched.

"'Tin Roof Blues'": The naturalist alluded to is Henry Beston whose *Herbs and the Earth* supplies the quoted phrase.

The Autumn House Poetry Series

Michael Simms, General Editor

OneOnOne Jack Myers

Snow White Horses Ed Ochester

The Leaving Sue Ellen Thompson

Dirt Jo McDougall

Fire in the Orchard Gary Margolis

Just Once, New and Previous Poems Samuel Hazo

The White Calf Kicks Deborah Slicer • 2003, selected by Naomi Shihab Nye

The Divine Salt Peter Blair

The Dark Takes Aim Julie Suk

Satisfied with Havoc Jo McDougall

Half Lives Richard Jackson

Not God After All Gerald Stern

Dear Good Naked Morning Ruth L. Schwartz • 2004, selected by Alicia Ostriker

A Flight to Elsewhere Samuel Hazo

Collected Poems Patricia Dobler

The Autumn House Anthology of Contemporary American Poetry
    Sue Ellen Thompson, ed.

Déjà Vu Diner Leonard Gontarek

lucky wreck Ada Limón • 2005, selected by Jean Valentine

The Golden Hour Sue Ellen Thompson

Woman in the Painting Andrea Hollander Budy

Joyful Noise: An Anthology of American Spiritual Poetry Robert Strong, ed.

No Sweeter Fat Nancy Pagh • 2006, selected by Tim Seibles

Unreconstructed: Poems Selected and New Ed Ochester

Rabbis of the Air Philip Terman

The River Is Rising Patricia Jabbeh Wesley

Let It Be a Dark Roux Sheryl St. Germain

Dixmont Rick Campbell

The Dark Opens Miriam Levine • 2007, selected by Mark Doty

The Song of the Horse Samuel Hazo

• Winner of the annual Autumn House Poetry Prize
* *Coal Hill Review* chapbook series

DESIGN AND PRODUCTION

Cover and text design by Chiquita Babb

Cover art: Harnett, William Michael, *The Old Violin*, 1886, oil on canvas. Gift of Mr. and Mrs. Richard Mellon Scaife in honor of Paul Mellon. Image courtesy National Gallery of Art, Washington.

Author photograph: Matthew Gibb

Text set in Weiss, a font designed by Emil Rudolf Weiss in 1926, based on typefaces from the Italian Renaissance

Printed by McNaughton & Gunn on 60# Natural Offset Eggshell